Assertiveness Training:

10 Simple Steps How to Become an Assertive Leader, Stand Up, speak up, and Take Control of Your Life

Table of Contents

Introduction......5

Step 1: Manage Expectations......7

Step 2: Consider Your Means of Expression......14

Step 3: Use Assertive Communication Techniques......20

Step 4: Break Negative Personal Patterns.......25

Step 5: Improve Self-Confidence......33

Step 6: Change Your Mindset......39

Step 7: Improve Your Emotional Intelligence......51

Step 8: Improve Your Understanding of Body Language......62

Step 9: Practice Assertive Body Language......72

Step 10: Fake It Until You Make It......79

Conclusion......84

© Copyright 2018 by Luke Caldwell - All rights reserved.

The follow eBook is reproduced below with the goal of providing information that is as accurate and reliable as possible. Regardless, purchasing this eBook can be seen as consent to the fact that both the publisher and the author of this book are in no way experts on the topics discussed within and that any recommendations or suggestions that are made herein are for entertainment purposes only. Professionals should be consulted as needed prior to undertaking any of the action endorsed herein.

This declaration is deemed fair and valid by both the American Bar Association and the Committee of Publishers Association and is legally binding throughout the United States.

Furthermore, the transmission, duplication or reproduction of any of the following work including specific information will be considered an illegal act irrespective of if it is done electronically or in print. This extends to creating a secondary or tertiary copy of the work or a recorded copy and is only allowed with express written consent from the Publisher. All additional right reserved.

The information in the following pages is broadly considered to be a truthful and accurate account of facts and as such any inattention, use or misuse of the information in question by the reader will render any resulting actions solely under their purview. There are no scenarios in which the publisher or the original author of this work can be in any fashion deemed liable for any hardship or damages that may befall them after undertaking information described herein.

Additionally, the information in the following pages is intended only for informational purposes and should thus be thought of as universal. As befitting its nature, it is presented without assurance regarding its prolonged validity or interim quality. Trademarks that are mentioned are done without written consent and can in no way be considered an endorsement from the trademark holder.

Introduction

Congratulations on downloading *Assertiveness Training: 10 Simple Steps How to Become The Person You Meant to Be, Self-Expression, Speak up, Stand Up For Yourself Without Being Arrogant And Take Control of Your Own Life* and thank you for doing so. Making the decision to stop being a passive observer in your life and taking control of it by asserting yourself is a big decision and one for which you should be applauded.

Unfortunately, it is also the easiest step in the process which is why the following steps will discuss everything you need to know to improve your ability to be assertive when the need arises, without stepping over the line and enforcing your will on anyone else in an aggressive manner. First, you will learn all about what being assertive is, as well as what it is not so that you can move forward with a clear understanding of what is in store. Next, you will learn tricks for expressing yourself in an assertive manner through a variety of different communication techniques.

You will then learn how to pick out the negative patterns that are holding you back from being as assertive as you might otherwise be, how to improve your mindset and enhance your self-confidence. From there you will learn to read other peoples emotions by improving your emotional intelligence and also learn to read their body language and control your own. Finally, you will learn how to fake an assertive attitude successfully until you develop your own.

There are plenty of books on this subject on the market, thanks again for choosing this one! Every effort was made to ensure it is full of as much useful information as possible, please enjoy!

IF YOU LIKE THIS BOOK, REVIEW IS ALWAYS MUCH APPRECIATE ☺

Step 1: Manage Expectations

When it comes to learning to be assertive, everyone is going to come to the task with a different mindset and different expectations as to what the end result will be. As such, the first step to becoming a more assertive individual is understanding just what assertiveness is and what it is not.

Unfortunately, what is and what is not assertive behavior is often muddled by the fact that, if you aren't careful, you can easily overstep the line and end up being seen as aggressive rather than assertive. A person who is assertive when it comes

to their needs is admired, a person who is aggressive for these same things is seen as a menace. Despite the serious differences between the two, it is still easy to confuse them, especially for those who are still learning about the finer points of assertiveness. As such, a definition of the two is useful in telling one from the other.

Assertiveness: At its heart, assertiveness is all about balance. It requires that you be in tune with yourself in order to accurately determine your wants and needs beforehand so that you can compare them to the wants and needs of those you come into contact with. Those who are assertive are self-assured and confident and use that inner strength to get their point across in a way that can be seen as both fair and empathetic to the other person's point of view.

Aggressiveness: Aggressive behavior, on the other hand, is completely based around winning. Those who are aggressive rather than assertive are going to do what is in their own best interest without any thought for the desires, feelings, needs, and rights of others. Those who are aggressive use the personal power they might have for selfish gains and are often seen as bullying or pushy by others. They take what they want, when they want it and damn the consequences.

Comparative example: For example, it's Friday afternoon and your boss suddenly drops a pile of new work on your desk and says it needs to be done ASAP. They are being aggressive in asking and, regardless of how important the work is, you are most likely going to resent them for it. They are disregarding your needs and feelings in favor of their own.

On the contrary, when you tell your boss in a firm but polite tone that you would be happy to do the work first thing Monday morning, you are being assertive. By telling them the work will be done you are appearing passive, while still setting boundaries in an assertive fashion that doesn't leave room for argument. You are asserting your own rights while also acknowledging the work needs to be done.

Drawing the line: While there is now doubt that being assertive is going to help improve your life in countless ways over the years, it is important to keep in mind that it is not going to be appropriate at all times. This is especially true in the workplace when some cultures will expect workers to be passive and even a hint of assertiveness is seen as rude or even downright offensive. When faced with this type of situation you will have to weigh your options and decide if the job is worth the way you are being treated.

You should also keep in mind that gender can play a serious role in how your assertive behavior is received. It is an unfortunate truth that men are often rewarded for assertiveness while women are punished for it. While this is not true in all situations it may be worth keeping in mind before you change your behavior too dramatically.

Regardless of your sex, drawing the line between behavior that is assertive and behavior that is aggressive is a difficult proposition. Early on, when preparing to assert yourself it is perfectly natural for you to second-guess yourself and wonder if you will do more harm than good. This will change over time, however, as you get to know the right times to stand up for yourself and the right times to hold your tongue. You can also find that this tightrope is easier to walk if you improve your ability to read the body language of others as well as sense their emotional intent via an increased emotional intelligence, both of which are discussed in detail in later steps.

In the workplace: In the workplace, everyone admires those who are assertive and can easily put forth their views and needs in a confident and direct way that gets results. They are known to stand up for themselves and respected for always taking the feels of others into account. Those who express aggressive behavior in the workplace, on the other hand, often look like Neanderthal, with those with the biggest clubs walking around and taking what they want, beating their chests at one another in an effort to see who's the strongest.

Now there are exceptions to the rule, of course, and type A aggressive personalities can certainly thrive in certain positions, especially sales. There is a limit here too, of course, but they can go much further before it's noticed. These forceful, aggressive individuals often dominate the workplace and sap everyone's morale with just a few words. This approach is always going to backfire in the end as no one can ever really trust the person who is aggressive.

Additional distinctions: If you constantly feel the need to fight fire with fire, then you are likely an aggressive individual and may find it hard to take a more measured, assertive path. Likewise, if you find yourself constantly making demands or having expectations that can never seem to be reached, then you may be aggressive rather than assertive as well.

On the other hand, if you make claims as opposed to demands in a poised, reasonable fashion, then you are likely already on the right track. Remember, a diplomatic, gentle nudge will allow the other party to make the first move and may likely cause them to respect you more as well. This is a sign of a true leader, someone who is assertive but not aggressive.

Watch those around you: One of the biggest differences between aggressiveness and assertiveness is the approach you take, which is why emotional intelligence is a key part of maximizing your assertiveness and why it has its own step later in this book. It is important to always watch your timing when you are planning to be assertive, and also to watch the reactions of those around you while you do so. You will also need to be aware of your personal patterns and any larger patterns as well, which you will learn more about in Step 4.

If you are doing something that previously hasn't resulted in success previously, then rather than being angry about this fact and taking an aggressive stance, it is often better to reassess the situation and move forward in a more appropriate fashion. Generally speaking, it will be better to slowly dole out what you are planning so you can gauge the reactions of those listening rather than betting it all and risking a scenario where you crash and burn. As with many things in life, the way you pitch your information is often going to be more important than the content in question.

Consider the question of confidence: While being confident is a prerequisite for being assertive, it is also important to consider how you appear to others if you choose to not be assertive. While not always the case, after a certain point you will begin to look timid for not pushing back. When you find yourself in this type of position then a good rule of thumb is often going to be waiting for your turn to speak, acknowledge what the other person is saying and then sticking to your guns. Regardless of the setting, you find yourself in, the other person is always going to be more receptive to what you have to say if you acknowledge their thoughts and opinions first.

While being defensive is going a perfectly natural reaction when an idea you believe to be valid is rejected, the fact of the matter is that this type of mindset is rarely going to get you anywhere. This is why acknowledging the other party's response is so important as it helps to build a consensus and thus to build trust as well. The only way you will get the other person to walk away feeling as though they ended up with a win-win scenario is if you can learn to compromise while still getting what you wanted. Doing so is the pinnacle of being assertive rather than aggressive.

Step 2: Consider Your Means of Expression

Understand that you cannot control the behavior of others: When it comes to developing a habit of being assertive in appropriate moments, one of the first things you will need to come to terms with is the fact that you can't truly control other people's behavior. As much as you may wish this was not the case, you can't just wave a magic wand and have the other person magically agree with you, regardless of how persuasive you may be. Once you understand that being assertive is more than bending people to your will then you can really get to work on improving yourself once and for all.

While it can be unfortunate that you can't control the behaviors of others in some situations, it is also freeing in a way as it also means that you don't need to take on the burden of accepting responsibility for the way other people respond to your assertiveness either. Assuming you approach them in a respectful, calm manner then it is not your fault if they respond in a resentful or angry fashion, no matter what they may say at the moment.

The truth is they are likely dealing with personal or professional issues that are outside of your ken and they have no bearing on whether or not your being assertive was the right choice in the situation. As long as you then control your response to their response and aren't actively violating the other party's needs with your request then you have the right to say and do as you please.

Consciously place more value on yourself: In order to ensure that assertiveness ends up eventually being your natural response in appropriate situations, it is vital that you not only have what you would consider being a good understanding of yourself, but also a strong understanding of your personal value and worth as a human being, and also to whomever you are trying to be assertive. It is this self-belief that will ultimately go on to become self-confidence, and ultimately lead to assertive behavior. It will also make it easier for you to recognize when someone isn't treating you with the dignity and respect that you deserve and stand up and do what needs to be done when you see this occur. Ultimately this will make it far easier for you to remain true to yourself and your needs and wants.

However, it is also extremely important that you don't take this newfound self-belief to the extremes as, if so, you can end up placing your less important needs over the more important needs of others. While it is certainly true that your desires, needs, feelings and thoughts are as important as anyone else's they are certainly not more important, and if you treat them as such then you are no longer just assertive you have slipped into full on aggressive.

Voice your wants and needs the right way: If you are going to be the best version of yourself that you can be then you are going to need to ensure that your vital wants and needs are met. The first step to doing so successful is understanding that no one else is going to do this for you. You have no guarantees that they are going to even recognize your needs, much less meet them of their own accord. It is vital that you take the initiative in these scenarios and identify what you want and what you need to get it and then make your plans known.

After you have completed this process you can then tell those in a position to help you or to stand in your way what it is that you are ultimately going to need from them in order to reach your goals. As you will be extremely sure about the specifics, you will thus be able to express them in a clear and confident way that will be more likely to see results than what might otherwise be the case. Even if what you need isn't currently possible, asking for it now in an assertive fashion will make it easier to bring up again when the time is right.

As you will know the ins and outs of the situation in question at this point, you will also find that it is easier for you to get what you want without sacrificing the needs of others to get them. Remember, your assertiveness is going to be rewarded with success much more frequently if you frame it in such a way that the other party can get away with doing as little work as possible.

Be positive: While it may seem like a small thing, if you assert yourself with a positive spin you are far more likely to see success than if you leave things neutral. What's worse, if you assert yourself with a depressed or angry tone then you are likely to come off as aggressive even if you said the exact same thing. Instead, it is always best to approach the situation in a sensitive and constructive manner in order to see the best results. Don't be afraid to stand up for yourself when you feel your rights are being infringed upon but take care to remain respectful and control your emotions at all times.

Don't reject criticism outright: Many people make the mistake of assuming that assertiveness means never listening to criticism, but in reality, this is an aggressive mentality that isn't sustainable in the long-term. Instead, it is still important to accept negative as well as positive feedback as positively, humbly and graciously as possible. Even if you don't agree with the criticism, listening to it is going to give you a better idea of what the other party's grievances are, which will then make it easier for you to decide how you are going to come up with a compromise that works for everyone.

Practice saying no: If you are working hard to improve your assertiveness then odds are you also have a difficult time saying no. This is one of the most basic steps required in order to become truly assertive, however, as without this ability you will never be able to stop aggressive people from walking right over you. One of the best ways to get started breaking this habit is understanding that there is no way you will be able to please everyone or do everything that you would like to do. As such, saying no is inevitable and it is far preferable to determine when you are going to do so as opposed to letting it happen at random when you finally finish taking on more than you can handle.

Step 3: Use Assertive Communication Techniques

Use more "I" statements: Statements like "I feel," or "I want" allow you to get your point across in a clear and effective way. What's more, by making sure to include the word "I", you make it clear to the other person that you understand that perception is relative and that their viewpoint is as valid as your own. Additionally, it will help you to keep the facts separate from what you want out of a given scenario which will help ensure you come to the best outcome possible as well.

Escalate in the right way: If you find that your initial attempt at being assertive fails, then you may need to escalate things further to get your point across. This may include taking a tone that is as firm as possible while still remaining respectful and polite at the same time. This is not to say that you are going to escalate the emotional intensity of the situation, as you will end up coming off aggressive if this is the case. Learning how to walk this line may only happen with practice, which is why it is important to get out there and practice as much as possible until you learn to walk that tightrope successfully.

Try scripting: This technique is useful for those who are just getting started when it comes to being assertive as it allows you to work out what you are going to say in advance so there isn't any question as to what to do next at the moment. In order to construct the right thing to say, the first thing you are going to want to focus on is the event. This includes a breakdown of exactly how you see the current problem or situation and ensures you can both work from the same baseline.

Next, you will need to consider how the situation makes you feel and also how you can express this fact while at the same time making it sound as though you are blaming the other party for anything. Making your feelings clear is the only way you can express to the other party how important it is that a change is made, which is what you will express by talking about your needs. This will ensure the other party knows exactly what you need from them so that there are no misunderstandings and they can choose a response without having to guess at your meaning. Finally, you will want to indicate what the results of your request will be, either the benefits of going along with your plan or the consequences of not going ahead with your plan, whichever is more persuasive.

Don't be afraid to feel anger: One of the biggest obstacles that many people face when learning to communicate in an assertive fashion is the idea that expressing anger while being assertive is akin to being aggressive. This does not have to be the case, as long as you express your anger in a way that is free from the negative trappings that are often associated with it, however, as what is often wrong with anger is the way people express it, not that it is felt in the first place. Understanding that you deserve to have your feelings, whatever they may be, is an important part of truly becoming assertive.

Make your requests as clear as possible: In order to ensure that expressing your assertiveness is met with as much success as possible, it is important to ensure you take the time to craft requests that are as clear and rational as possible. A truly assertive request is going to be straightforward while also taking care to not deprecate the other person in the process. This is in direct contrast to the passive aggressive requests that many people regularly make that are design to hurt the other party in one way or another while at the same time being easily deniable.

Provide validation: Another part of being able to make an assertive request without coming across as aggressive is to take the time to understand what feelings the other person is trying to express so that you can make it clear that you understand were they are coming from. This is different than agreeing with them, however, and will simply make them feel as though their concerns are being heard while allowing you to still move forward in a more productive fashion.

While listening to what they have to say it is important to ensure you maintain both a verbal and nonverbal attitude of respect and openness in order to help the other person feel as open with you as possible. To help further the cause you will also want to always maintain eye contact. While listening you are going to want to put aside any personal biases you might have in an attempt to find the solution that is truly best for the task at hand.

Step 4: Break Negative Personal Patterns

When it comes to successfully setting off down the path to the type of change that you are trying to cultivate long-term, it is important to consider the various nonproductive patterns you find yourself returning to time and again. These patterns are likely all around you, both in your personal behavior and in the behavior of those around you and if you really want to see change in your overall level of assertiveness, then recognizing them *before* you interact with them is crucial to moving forward once and for all.

You are in luck, however, as just like being assertive, pattern recognition is a skill which means that you can eventually master it if you put in the work to do so. This doesn't necessarily mean it is going to be a quick process, however, which is why it is best to get started as quickly as possible. The following tips will help you get started off on the right foot.

Realize the patterns all around you: Before you can get started picking out your negative personal patterns, you will likely find that looking at the patterns of the world around you will help to put you in the type of mindset you are looking to cultivate. After you know what to look for, you will then find natural and manmade patterns practically all around you at all times. You can find patterns in everything from the way the leaves cast shadows on a tree to the cracks in the sidewalk and the way people interact with one another when confronted with the same set of stimuli.

Only once you start seeing these basic patterns more regularly, you will then find that the more abstract and complex variations start making themselves known to you as well. This means you are going to want to try and see the patterns in the behaviors of the people you interact with most frequently. Only by being able to accurate determine the types of patterns that are taking place around you at all time will you be able to understand how these patterns intersect will you be able to turn this knowledge inwards and see the personal patterns that are keeping you from reaching the level of success you are waiting for.

If you find that you have a relatively easy time of seeing the patterns of others without clearly finding your own, the best place to start is with those things that you can clearly count on to happen each and every day. Once you start seeing the small things that happen like clockwork you can then move on to bigger and bigger series of cause and effect until you can eventually determine the cause and effect of everything around you. Don't worry if you can't find all of the information that you need in order to make all the required logical connections, making sense of everything at this point isn't nearly as important as noting the inconsistencies that you come across for further study later. Noticing all of these different types of patterns is ultimately the first step when it comes to breaking negative patterns once and for all.

Group the patterns together: Taking note of as many different patterns as possible is crucial as a first step as the next step is going to be groping patterns together based on how they fit together and how they affect once another. This should allow you to determine more easily how your personal patterns relate to larger patterns overall and also the similarities between your personal patterns and those that you see around you. Take care not to group things that are only tangentially associated with one another is only going to skew the data, even if it does make it easier to keep track of anything. Don't be afraid to write things down and to take your time.

You will also need to leave yourself open to the fact that it is possible that you were wrong about some of your initial assumptions about patterns, which means you need to be willing to make changes to your conclusions as you move along. You may also come across new patterns you were previously aware of and may need to fit them into the framework as well. Before moving on from this phase it is important that you have a clear understanding of the big picture that works for you. It is only when you reach this point that you will be able to make an informed decisions about how to best move forward in the shortest period of time possible.

Look for other patterns to change: After you have a better understanding of the patterns that you are looking at, and which are negatively affecting you, you can then start to decide what needs to be changed for the greatest overall result along with the ones that you decide you need to hold onto no matter what. Of course, changing personal patterns is easier said than done, especially with those that have been around for decades. Planning is key at this juncture as it will be extremely easy for you to slip up and fall back into your old habits with really even thinking about it.

For example, imagine a scenario where you constantly take on more work than you should as a way of avoiding the need to be assertive. Once you became aware of this pattern you could then make a concentrated effort to focus your assertiveness efforts towards things that will cause you to take on more than your fair share of the work but also by working more closely with your coworkers to devise a more effective means of dolling out tasks so that it doesn't fall on one person to pick up the slack in the first place.

Once you have decided on the patterns that you want to focus on changing, it is extremely important that you follow through on them or risk derailing the effectiveness of this entire process. If you try to change a troublesome pattern, fail and then give up, you are only creating a new, even worse pattern where you retreat from patterns that know are harmful. As such, it is important to start with an easy pattern to change to ensure that you can get into the proper swing of things. Additionally, it is important to be aware that it is going to take more than making a new plan to change any patterns that are deeply ingrained, but it will also take commitment, dedication and a state of extreme vigilance to ensure that once you have it mastered, the pattern stays gone for good.

Generally speaking, if you are hoping to change a negative pattern, the best choice is to completely replace it with a more productive one instead. The new pattern will need to avoid any of the triggers that lead to the original pattern, however, so it is important to plan out new habits and not to simply glom onto the first thing that comes along that helps you avoid the negative pattern.

It will typically take about a month for a new pattern to completely supplant the old one which means that minor instances of failure are to be expected as you get into the new swing of things. Nevertheless, it is vital that you don't use minor instances of failure as an excuse to revert even more thoroughly back to your old, negative habits. Sticking to the new pattern right away isn't the goal, that will come with time, when you first start any deviation from the old pattern should be seen as a victory.

Negative patterns: While you are taking stock of your common patterns, you are naturally going to want to flag those that are going to make it more difficult for you to continue making positive changes in the future. Additionally, you will want to be on the lookout for patterns that tend to demand instant gratification as they too will make it more difficult for you to make all the changes you need to make in order to be the master of assertiveness you can eventually be. Additionally, while the saying ignorance is bliss is true in some situations, this isn't one of them, make a habit of stamping out any patterns that promote ignorance ASAP.

Another very important pattern to avoid if you ever hope to be assertive on the fly is a desire for a strong level of control over everything around you, no matter what. While taking control of your life is obviously an important part of making the types of long-term changes you are striving for, if you need to control every aspect of a situation then you will never really get anywhere.

This can often tie into patterns related to the flight or fight instinct, especially if you find yours is skewed to far in the flight direction. Don't forget, balance is crucial to ensuring this response doesn't harm your ability to ensure positive change which means you may need to watch your gut reaction to conflict and then work to balance it as needed.

Positive patterns: While culling your negative patterns, it is important to stop and take the time to be aware of the positive patterns that you have developed over time as well. With all the deep dives into your negative patterns, it can be easy to get down on yourself and feel as though you will never make it to where you need to be. This is when a list of your positive patterns will come in handy as it will serve to remind you of what you have gotten right so far as well. Not only that but becoming more aware of the positive patterns that you are a part of will also make it easier for you to actively take steps to enhance and expand upon them as well.

Doing so will ultimately make it easier for you to change certain negative patterns and develop all new ones as you will also learn what type of challenges you can easily overcome and also those that you will need to focus on more directly if you ever hope to make any real progress. Overall, the most important types of habits that you can cultivate to improve your assertiveness are going to be loving yourself and feeling as though you deserve this type of positive change.

Additionally, you are going to want to keep a sharp eye out for patterns that promote a growth mindset based on expecting positive results to come from positive actions. Finally, other worthwhile positive actions include being aware of personal boundaries, those that don't need to change as well as those that do, and also patterns that promote being more in tune with your personal intuition in general.

Step 5: Improve Self-Confidence

The simple fact of the matter is that you can't ever expect to be truly assertive when the need arises until you have the confidence to believe in yourself no matter what. In order to help you get to where you need to be, consider the following tips.

Consider the true source of your fears
When it comes time to be assertive, if you find yourself becoming unreasonably afraid instead, the first thing you will need to do is to understand that the only way you will ever get over your fear of being assertive is if you completely master it. To help you move in that direction, consider the following tips that have work for countless others before you.

Reframe the anxiety: If you are uncertain how someone is going to respond to your assertiveness then it is possible for that uncertainty to manifest itself as anticipation. From there, it doesn't take much for anticipation to turn into fear and suddenly the thought of being assertive just became far less manageable. Reacting with fear in a scenario that requires self-confidence will only end up destroying the momentum that you may have developed in the conversation up to that point and mentally put you back to square one.

In order to nip your fear in the bud, you can use what is known as cognitive reframing. To use it in this scenario you would essentially trick your mind into viewing the fear of moving forward with a curiosity as to the results. Curiosity and self-confidence are a much better fit than fear and self-confidence and it can help you hold onto your momentum until the task is complete.

Consider what it is that you are actually afraid of: If you find yourself always reacting to scenarios where you can be assertive with the same fear response then you may want to dig a little deeper and consider why it is that you have found yourself in this unproductive loop. To extricate yourself from this pattern, the next time you come across a scenario where you start to become frightened by the idea of being assertive, rather than running from the fear you should attempt to lean into it and determine what it is that you are really afraid of. If you can't come up with a concrete reason as to why you should be afraid then you can press forward with confidence born from the fact that it likely doesn't exist.

Consider the worst thing that could happen
Until you have shown your mind that nothing bad is going to happen when you express your assertiveness, then it is just going to keep throwing up roadblocks to your success under the guise of preventing you from doing something dangerous. These roadblocks will often manifest themselves in a wide variety of increasingly outlandish scenarios that could potentially occur if you take the most assertive course of action possible. While these may be convincing at the moment, they are very rarely based on reality and that is how you can learn to avoid them.

Instead of letting your mind come up with potential scenarios that might occur were you to be assertive, you should stop for a moment and think critically about what the outcome is likely to be. Don't forget, most people are at the center of their own universe which means something that seems extremely important to you is likely to barely register if your lucky. With that in mind, odds are the worst case scenario you can come up with isn't going to be all that bad. If that still doesn't seem to be enough to get you out there and committing assertive acts, then you can try the following tricks as well.

Think of it as an experiment: If you still can't get over your fear of being assertive, then you may find success moving forward if you look at each opportunity to be assertive as a type of science experiment. If you are so certain that you understand what the negative outcome is going to be, then the only choice you have is to test it and see if your mind and all its extraneous outcomes were correct. This should also help to move your mindset more towards one of curiosity and then when things go in your favor, it will provide concrete evidence that being assertive isn't as scary as you previously thought.

Play the odds: If you never try to be as assertive as you want to be, then you will never succeed in doing the things that you associate with those who are assertive. Likewise, if you never put all of your assertiveness training into action then you will never even have the potential to come out on top. As such, at the very least you owe it to yourself to try being assertive at least a few times, just to see what will happen. After all, like they say in Las Vegas, you can't win if you never play.

Stop thinking about it: Thinking about all the ways that being more self-confident will help you in the future may take your mind off the present, but it won't do much to get you started when it comes to improving your day-to-day interactions with others. At some point, you need to put your new and improved thoughts into actions.

When it comes to stretching beyond your comfort zone, it is undoubtedly going to be difficult at first, but that is going to be true of anything. What's more, you should take some small comfort in the fact that while it is difficult for you, it was also just as difficult for everyone else who is now effortlessly assertive as assertiveness is a skill which means the only way you can ever hope to improve is with practice.

Stand up for yourself
When it comes to learning to express your self-confidence in appropriate and effective ways, standing up for yourself in verbal and physical situations will make it easier for you to learn to project your new confidence effectively while also making it easier for you to repeat the feat time and again in the future. Taking every possible opportunity to practice your new skills is always

recommended as this is the only guaranteed way of improving as much as possible.

The way you naturally interact with those around you is clearly going to be a direct reflection of the amount of self-confidence you feel on a regular basis. After you are ready to begin projecting your new mindset, it is important to be assertive while at the same time not taking things so far they slip into overly aggressive and you become part of the problem rather than the solution. Being assertive means expressing your own needs and desires and doing what is required to achieve them without directly forcing others to give in to your whims at the expense of their own personal goals. If you avoid speaking up when others are suppressing your happiness, then you are sabotaging any other attempts you might be making at improving your ability to believe in yourself.

Step 6: Change Your Mindset

By this point in the process, you should be well on your way to affecting a change in your overall level of assertiveness that allows you to get what you want out of a given situation without leaving the other person feeling bullied as a result. If you are still having a hard time breaking out of your old patterns, however, then perhaps your ability to be assertive isn't the issue. In fact, you could be dealing with a limiting mindset that will continually make it difficult to move forward in a productive fashion until it has been dealt with once and for all.

Two distinct mindsets
In fact, there are two distinct ways to view the idea of intelligence or ability, they can be seen as things which are innate which means what we are born with is all we ever get or they can be seen as skills that can be gained through effort and lots of hard work. These two different viewpoints, in turn, lead to drastically different behaviors which over time lead to drastically different results. If you head out into the world each day with the idea that you can improve and succeed at whatever you attempt, then you will find that success starts coming easier to you over time. This is what is referred to as a growth mindset and it is one of the main distinguishing characteristics of successful people.

As children, some people are told they excel in certain subjects while others are told that they succeeded because they tried hard and that effort leads to success. The first group of children can be expected to develop a fixed mindset whereby their brains become more active when they are being told how well they have done. The second group of children can be said to have a growth mindset wherein their minds are the most active when they are learning what they could do better next time. Those with a fixed mindset tend to worry more about how they are seen by others than what they are actually learning which is why those with a growth mindset tend to be more successful in the long run.

Fixed Mindset
- Wants to look smart or competent regardless of the reality
- Quick to avoid challenges
- Easily thwarted by obstacles
- Thinks effort is "pointless"
- Ignores feedback
- Can feel threatened by the success of others

Growth Mindset
- More interested in long-term results.
- Enjoys a challenge.

- Learns from obstacles
- Equates effort with success
- Appreciates criticism
- Finds inspiration in the success of others

To understand how the two mindsets work in action, simply remember the story of the tortoise and the hare. The hare was always told how fast he was and therefore developed a fixed mindset whereby his speed was innate and not related to his actions which meant he was free to take a nap during the race. The tortoise, on the other hand, kept a growth mindset which meant he knew that if he persevered he would succeed. This belief in himself was born out by the results of the race.

The two mindsets also manifest themselves differently when it comes to dealing with setbacks. When those who have a fixed mindset are met with a setback it directly affects how they see themselves because it shakes their belief in their innate talent. This makes it easier for them to give up on something they are struggling with as they can easily tell themselves that it is just not a talent that is in their wheelhouse. On the other hand, when a person with a growth mindset is met with a challenge they instead worry about the best way to overcome it and treat the issue as an opportunity to learn and grow.

Importance of neuroplasticity

If throughout the preceding examples you found yourself identifying more with the fixed mindset than the growth one, don't fret just yet. Neuroscientists have done studies proving that unlike much of ourselves, the human brain never stops changing and developing from childhood straight on through to old age. This is a result of a concept called neuroplasticity which refers to the brain's ability to reshape itself over time by creating new neural pathways. New pathways are added as new thoughts are repeated over time. As these thoughts persist they form patterns which are in turn used more frequently as neurons are more likely to travel down well-trod paths.

While this, in turn, means that it can be more difficult to change deeply ingrained habits, it also means that no mental or physical habit is so ingrained that it cannot be changed given enough time. Changing your way of thinking from a fixed mindset to a growth mindset may be one of the most difficult habits to break as it has been with you since childhood but it can be done if you put your mind to it. Here are a few tips to get you started:

- *Commit to the goal*: Changing your mind takes time and the only way you will see it through is to decide to bend all of your will to it from the start. Changing this set of neural pathways will take time, and dedication is the only way to see the change through.

- *Start small*: Seeing positive change as a result of new choices is one of the quickest ways to establish new neural pathways. To help get the idea of a growth mindset stuck in your brain, start with small changes which have easily perceivable results and use these results to bolster future success.
- *Be aware of your thoughts*: Take the time to inventory your life and note when your response to something comes from a thought that is born from a fixed mindset. Mentally flag those scenarios so that when they occur in the real world you can replace them with thoughts conducive to a growth mindset.

Rewire your brain

If you are looking for ways to be successful, the first thing you must do is determine what bad habits you currently enable so that you can begin to do something about them. Once you have taken the time to study your bad habits you can more easily determine where it stems from and therefore how you might begin to counteract it. One excellent way to become aware of your negative habits is to try meditation which is discussed in detail later in this step.

Once you have determined what habits you need to break yourself of it will be time to teach your brain how to prefer new better habits over the old negative ones. How difficult this will prove to be will ultimately rely on a number of factors including how long you have enabled the bad habit and how attached your mind is to it. This process can be made easier through the sorts of repetition often found in affirmations and mantras and is discussed in detail later on in this step. The important thing to remember is that the more you repeat a positive action the more likely your brain is to believe it and the more likely your conscious mind will use it as a basis for future action.

Once you have successfully banished negative habits it will be time to replace them with positive ones. The human brain is capable of great things, so much so that forming new habits over time barely rates among them. To ensure that you form the proper sort of habits it is important to begin the process with the idea of your desired habit firmly in place. Start by asking yourself what you want the final result to be and really picture it, consider all the facets of the changed you and consider how to best make them a reality.

Once you have a final product in mind, ask yourself why you should change in such a fashion and what the ultimate benefits may ultimately be. It is important to set about changing habits with purpose, it will make the time spent doing so much more palatable. Make a list of the benefits of your current course of action and write them down in a place where you can see them easily if you get discouraged. Remember, repetition, repetition, repetition, if you don't' work on the change constantly, nothing will come of it.

Once you have begun to change your faulty habits it is important to have a broad understanding of how long the change will take. The easier the bad habit is to engage in the more difficult it will be to change which is why having a general idea of the timetable for such can make working through it much easier. During this time it will also be important to make a mental list of places or activities which trigger the bad habit and avoid them when at all possible. Finding yourself in a situation where you are face to face with the things which trigger your bad habit is a surefire way to slip up and fall back into old habits.

Ensuring that you stay motivated through the process of building new habits can be difficult but keeping your eye on the prize can make it easier. Once you have a timeline established for how long it should take to form new successful habits it is important to add milestones to the timetable that will help your mind equate the effort you are putting forth with the ultimate success you will achieve. Stay optimistic and enroll your family and friends to help you stick with it. Even the most difficult habits can be formed after ten weeks and likewise after this period of time whatever you are attempting will have become as much of a habit as it is every going to.

Affirmations and Mantras
In this instance, repetition is a useful way to bypass the fixed mindset filters that your brain has established over the years as a way to determine the best course of action in any given situation. Repetition is a great way to trick these filters into receiving new input without having to change them naturally. One way to do this is through the help of affirmations or mantras. An affirmation is a positive sentence which you take the time to write time and again throughout the day. A mantra basically the same thing but it is repeated throughout the day mentally instead. Affirmations and mantras are a great way to wean out background noise thoughts and effectively help retrain your brain and create new neural pathways. Some common affirmations or mantras include.
- Today, you are perfect
- Forward progress! Just keep moving!

- You are the sky
- I am attracting all the love I dream of and deserve
- Follow my path to happiness
- I am strong. I am beautiful. I am enough
- I am grateful for my life so far and for what is to come
- I am fulfilled
- Less is more

When you first begin using affirmations and mantras it is perfectly natural for the fixed mindset part of your brain to react negatively to the practice and cause you to doubt the process or feel foolish doing it. That is perfectly normal and in no way indicates how successful you will be at using a growth mindset to achieve success. You have spent years and years following a fixed mindset and this is simply an example of that mindset being put into practice. When thoughts like these appear use them as an opportunity to double down on the affirmation or mantra reminding yourself how much you really do believe in it. Ignore that part of your mind and it will grow quieter with time.

However, that is not to say that an affirmation or mantra that is radically different from where your conscious mind is currently at will suddenly change how you think, that is not how the conscious mind works. The conscious mind weighs personal experience heavily when deciding on a relevant course of action. From there it pulls in intellect and emotion to decide if a thought fits its predetermined course of action. What this means is that is best to start slowly when it comes to affirmations and mantras, if you try to do too much too fast you will end up not accomplishing much of anything.

Limiting beliefs
When choosing a realistic mantra or affirmation it is important to think carefully as they can cause real and meaningful changes to occur. That being said, do not be discouraged if you do not see many results even after diligently working at it for a month or more. Each person's mind has different levels of resistances to changing different mental processes and different process, in turn, take different amounts of time, keep at it and the results will come. Focusing purely on the results is not the most effective ways to use affirmations and mantras and this sort of mindset is indicative of the fixed mindset.

Changing your mindset effectively is about rewiring your brain to equate effort with results. For example, if you want to get in shape then try saying "I have the energy to exercise everyday instead of "I love the way I look". The first mantra can help you find the motivation to put the effort in and exercise regularly while the second hopes for some passive change to miraculously appear. The first is an example of the growth mindset and will help you improve your life and find success, the second is an example of a fixed mindset that is just waiting for success to find them.

If you find it difficult to put forth mantras or affirmations that focus on actions and not results, then it might be beneficial to look inward and determine what thoughts are keeping you from thinking positively. To take the exercise example from earlier a step further, say that you are interested in exercising regularly but you can't find an affirmation or mantra that seems to fit. This could be because you have needed to lose weight all of your life or you have tried to exercise regularly and then failed but it doesn't matter now. Focusing on the past will only enhance negative neural pathways and make any additional forward progress that much harder. Once you have pinpointed the negative thoughts interfering with your affirmations and mantras it is time to let them go by focusing on the future, not the past.

Beliefs that cannot be let go of so easily can instead be changed over time by layering them with transformative and empowering thoughts instead. If you bury your old negative thoughts under enough positive thoughts eventually the negative ones won't be able to get out. Start with affirmations and mantras that reflect the change. Say things like "I am becoming more successful" or "I am consistently taking positive action to move forward".

Successfully creating appropriate affirmations and mantras is about knowing yourself and your strengths and weaknesses. For some goals, you will find you have half a dozen limiting beliefs while for others you might find only a single one. As you think about different goals that the time to listen to what reasons for abandoning it pop up in your head, these are your limiting beliefs.

Step 7: Improve Your Emotional Intelligence

Just because you are learning to be assertive, doesn't mean it should be your default response in every situation, after all, there are always going to be times when the better choice is to let the other person have their way. If you are new to being assertive, however, it is easy for it to feel like the right tool for every situation. If this sounds like you then you could benefit from spending some time improving your emotional intelligence.

While not discussed nearly as regularly as traditional intelligence, emotional intelligence is just as important to everyday life as it makes it easier for you to turn thoughts into actions, make worthwhile connections with others and will generally ensure you make better decisions where other people are concerned. More specifically, emotional intelligence is the ease with which you are able to access your own emotions, understand what they are really trying to tell you and also manage and identify a wide variety of situations, including those that require you to make an empathetic connection with others, communicate succinctly or assert yourself without coming off as overly aggressive. Emotional intelligence will also make it easier to understand the nonverbal cues the other person might be giving off which will be discussed in detail in the next step.

In order to maximize your emotional intelligence as quickly as possible, the first thing you need to do is consider where you are currently at as far as your emotional intelligence is concerned. To do so, consider the level of quality when it comes to your performance in the following areas:

Workplace: The workplace is full of complex social interactions that can be complicated to see clearly at the best of times and if your emotional intelligence isn't where you would like it to be then you likely find yourself routinely baffled by why those around you seem to walk on eggshells around certain people. Improving your emotional intelligence will allow you to motivate others and stand out to the point where a promotion to management is the next logical step. This is true to the point where many businesses are now as interested in emotional intelligence as they are traditional intelligence.

Your overall health: Emotional intelligence easily allows you to understand your own emotions more completely, which naturally makes them easier to manage as well. This, in turn, means it will also make it easier for you to manage your stress levels without issue which will lead to a lower risk of infertility, cardiovascular disease, blood pressure, stroke and an all around weakening of the immune system. This goes beyond your physical health as well as if left untreated, higher than average levels of stress can lead to depression, anxiety and even more severe mental problems. The reoccurring failure to connect with others can even ultimately lead to suicidal thoughts.

The way you interact with others: The more easily you can understand your emotions, the more easily you can understand the emotions of others. This, in turn, makes your interpersonal relationships flow more smoothly, while also helping you to understand the way others are feeling so you can best assert yourself without stepping on anyone's toes. The relationships formed as a result of a high emotional intelligence also allow for more mutually beneficial relationships to form.

Improving your EQ

EQ is made up of four parts which all build on one another, but function perfectly well on their own as well. Taking advantage of them as fully as possible is the key to true success.

Self-assurance: In order to successfully improve your emotional intelligence, you will need to come to a fresh understanding of the emotions you are feeling in the moment and also understand how those emotions are going to ultimately influence your actions as well. True self-awareness starts with self-assessment and you should pay special attention to the emotional impulses that you are aware of but that you currently have a difficult time controlling as well as those you can already handle.

If you don't know where to begin, the first thing you should do is keep a journal describing the experiences you have each day and how they make you feel. It is important to be as detail and unbiases in these journal entries as possible as you can later use it as a record of where you started and how far you have come. You can also use it to uncover personal patterns that you may not even have been aware existed. It is important to write down your experiences in a physical notebook, if possible, to ensure that your thoughts and emotions get the physical weight that they deserve. It is equally important to keep in mind that the physical reaction you have in response to your emotions, including things like stiffness in the neck, increase heartbeat and tension in the shoulders and write these symptoms of stress down as well.

You are going to want to make a point of only writing down you emotions at the end of each day as this will give you time to really reflect on each of the instances in question as opposed to writing them down so that they paint a specific picture or only show that you are making progress in a specific direction. Once you have a decent cross section of experiences that you have regularly you can begin to take note of similarities and difference in specific scenarios that may have ultimately led to different emotional responses or reactions to a response. Forewarned is forearmed and understanding how certain situations influence your future emotions will make it easier to start to manage them successfully.

Control: After you have come to a more complete understanding of your emotions, as well as the ways in which they are controlling the current scenario, the next thing you are going to need to do is to work on controlling your own emotions so they don't get in the way when it really matters most. Keep in mind, however, that this is something different than cutting yourself off from your emotions completely and is instead more about managing them appropriately and using what's available to you as constructively as possible. If you find yourself about to enter a potentially emotional scenario, do yourself a favor and take an extra 30 seconds to prepare for it beforehand by mentally defining the emotions you are likely to experience as well as the responses that you are likely going to face. This is the true first step to being able to properly take control of your emotions.

Once you are truly comfortable taking stock of your own emotions and responses, you should already be feeling more in control of your emotions as a result. Remember, don't cut your emotions off entirely, understand that everything has an appropriate time and outlet. Rather, your goal should instead be during this period to create as many new positive habits as possible to replace any negative reactions you previously experienced. If you find that this is still more easily said than done, consider the mentality you assume when giving your emotions some serious thought. If you find this to be easier said then done then perhaps you are thinking about your emotions incorrectly in the first place, you aren't the victim, you are the master.

If you feel as though your negative emotions are still leaving you with a number of unresolved stress, even while you still feel in control of them, then there are plenty of different options when it comes to dealing with that stress in an appropriate way and in what amounts to a healthy fashion. The most effective technique for many people is to simply focus on taking several long, deep breaths. This is an oldy but a goody as breathing too shallowly during times of stress will only amplify these feelings even more.

While practicing these breathing exercises you are going to want to also focus on actively relaxing your muscles, one muscle group at a time. Focusing on each muscle group and visualizing them releasing their stress is a great way to force your body to calm down as it is difficult for it to be relaxed in parts and stressed in others at the same time. Spend just a few minutes working over your entire body and you will be surprised how much better you suddenly feel.

Dealing with the emotions of others: After you have a firmer grasp on your own emotions and how they affect your behavior, you will find that it becomes much easier to register the emotions that other people are feeling as well and relate them directly to specific actions that may be experienced. During this phase, you will want to focus more on deciphering and noticing the clues they are presenting and then relating them back to the emotions you feel when you exhibit them so that you know where to start. When it comes to deal with assertiveness it is also important to consider any power dynamics that may be in play and the way they can be counted on to affect the situation as well.

In order to actively work on improving your overall social awareness, you will need to work on improving your overall level of empathy and also relating what you have already learned to those around you and making it clear you are participating in a given conversation without stepping into aggressive territory. While this might sound easy, it can be more complicated in practice which is why it is important to practice conveying the intention that you value the other person and their input in the conversation while still asserting your will over the conversation as a whole.

To do so, you will want to start by picturing the last few conversations you had with someone whom you didn't know terribly well, if at all. During the interaction did you take the time to put away distractions while the other person was speaking? Did you make eye contact for about 50 percent of the time while they were talking and most of the time while you were talking. Was the fact that you were interested in what was being discussed reflected in your body language?

As a general rule, you should always make a point of using body language that is open including not touching your face, not creating artificial barriers, laughing or smiling regularly, using lots of eye contact, not crossing your arms or legs and slightly leaning towards the other person. Without this, even if the things you are saying are pleasant, the only thing that will come across is how cold you seem.

It is also important to ensure that everyone is on the same page before the end of the conversation, which is also a great way to ensure that your assertiveness took hold in terms of influencing the conversation. This recap will ensure that you are both on the same page across the board, and also let you swoop in and change some last minute perceptions if required. While you may feel as though this makes it seem like you weren't listening, the truth of the matter is that it shows you value the other person's time by ensuring it won't be wasted dealing with simple miscommunication.

Nurture existing relationships: Once you have learned all you can about the emotional tells of those around you, it is now time to learn more about maintaining healthy relationships and expanding new potential interactions. You will also learn to inspire others to action by communicating clearly and diffusing potential conflict. If you hope to successfully manage relationships, then you need to use what you have learned to far in order to determine how you and the other party are affecting one another and what effect external forces are having on the scenario you now find yourself dealing with. Only by having a clear and accurate picture of all the moving pieces will you be able to find the right solution to please everyone.

Determining a true picture of the scenario will then allow you to determine more easily how to proceed based on the tools you have at your disposal. It is important to always get input from everyone involved and to take the time to accurately consider their emotional state in addition to listening to what they have to say. In fact, combining the two data streams would then allow you to get to the bottom of what they are really thinking, regardless of what they might be saying out loud. This way you will be able to work on determining a solution that is right for everyone in an assertive, not an aggressive, fashion.

After you have then come to a decision you will want to add an emotional appeal to your assertive approach to ensure they go along with the solution you proposed because they want to, not because they feel coerced. Making your empathy known is a great way to also make it clear that you are working towards something that will work to everyone's best interested, another surefire way to ensure your assertiveness is taken in the right way.

This can be a difficult task at times, but if you have been practicing then you should be up for the challenge.

When looking to improve your interpersonal relationships it is important to understand that it is a journey without an end. There is no magic point where a relationship doesn't require effort and upkeep, it should be a constant give and take. You will be aided by your improved emotional intelligence, however, and even if you don't always understand why the other person feels the way they do, you will at least be able to understand their emotions and where they, at least, are coming from.

Step 8: Improve Your Understanding of Body Language

If, despite your best efforts, you still don't seem to be on the same page with a person you are speaking with, despite trying to express yourself in a way that is assertive and not aggressive, then the issue in question might come down to body language. While this is not something that many people consider all that often, the fact of the matter is that nonverbal communication makes up a full 50 percent of every face to face interaction which means, at the very least, it bears thinking about when it comes to leaving a life of being timid behind you.

What's more, after you learn to read it properly, you will find that understanding the body language of those you meet will make it easier for you to interact with them in a way that allows you to be assertive while still taking their mental state into account. What's more, the other party may not be aware of all the information they are sharing, allowing you to plug directly into their subconscious so you know you are in tune with what they are really thinking.

Nonverbal communication includes things like facial expression, physical movements, breathing, gestures, perspiration and even the tone and the pitch of what's being said. While this is certainly a lot of additional information to process all at once, after you get used to doing so you will find that you are more able to easily control the ebb and flow of a conversation to steer it in the direction you are interested in going.

Of course, understanding the body language of others is only half the battle, and you will still nee to ensure that you are also giving off the proper body language cues when it comes to gesture, posture, tone, expression and eye contact. If you end up saying one thing while doing another, even accidentally, then the other party is going to naturally feel as though there is something off about the conversation, potentially ruining your ability to be assertive in the process. Learning to maximize the effectiveness of your personal body language is covered in the next step.

Types of nonverbal communication
When a person's nonverbal and verbal messages are on the same page, the effectiveness of what they are trying to say is compounded, taking your assertive statements and making them seem down right impossible to ignore. In fact, body language is able to affect the way you interact with others in

numerous different ways, each of which is outlined below. Understanding each will allow you to be aware of when they are present in others so you can react accordingly.

Reinforce: This type of nonverbal communication occurs when nonverbal cues and verbal cues align in such a way that they are in complete harmony with one another. These cues can then either serve to emphasize specific sections of an assertive statement or enhance the overall effectiveness of your message.

Undermine: If the nonverbal cues do not align, however, then they are only going to serve to undermine one another no matter how obviously truthful what is being said might be. If nonverbal cues don't align with verbal cues then most people are going to naturally assume that what is being said is deceitful and what is being expressed by body language is the true state of things. This is due to the fact it is assumed that nonverbal cues are linked directly to the subconscious which means they are trying to break through the lie that is being told.

Body language to watch

Face: It doesn't matter where you go or who you are speaking to, people around the world naturally make similar faces when exposed to similar stimuli. While not everyone is going to be extremely expressive, if you keep an eye on their faces then you are sure to see something slip now and then.

Movement and stance: The human brain is a big fan of first impressions as it makes it easy ready whatever is supposed to happen next. While all first impressions are not always going to be accurate, they often prove a surprisingly successful metric when it comes to determining the other person's intentions, especially when it comes to the way they stand and more. Even without practice, it should be easy to tell the difference between a relaxed stance and an anxious one and deduce the reasons this might be the case accordingly.

Hand movements: For more than 70 percent of the population the hand movements they make while speaking are going to be largely subconscious and will be made in reaction to the conversation or to add extra emphasis on the current topic of conversation. Either way, these gestures can prove an extremely useful tool when it comes to gauging how committed the other party is to your current topic of conversation. Hand gestures can be a little confusing at times as well, however, as they are not universal like facial expressions. This means that a gesture that is completely benign in your home country could be incredibly offensive somewhere else so it is important to do your research before heading abroad.

Eyes: Much like hand movements, where a person looks during a conversation is going to be a major indicator of how the conversation is going overall. While there are also local customs to consider, generally speaking avoiding eye contact is either seen as a sign of respect or a sign of guilt. On the other end of the spectrum, holding intense eye contact can be seen as either a sign of affinity or a sign of extreme attraction.

Physical location: When having a conversation with someone, it is important to ensure that you always allow them to dictate the space between you during the conversation. Doing so will allow you to use the amount of space as a barometer for how the conversation is going, making it easier for you to be assertive if the conversation requires it. The closer the other person stands to you the more they agree with what you are saying, while the reverse is also true. The same thing goes for any physical barriers they may put between you, or even if they are holding something that ends up forming a mental barrier between you if nothing else.

Tone and timber of voice: The tone and timber of the voice of the other party are just as important as the words they say. Simple things like pronunciation or emphasis can both make a serious difference in what is being said versus what is being meant and the same sentence can have countless variations as a result. Generally speaking, a calm, slightly stern tone indicates the other person is trying to take control of the conversation and speaking slightly to quietly for you to hear is a power play that is aimed at trying to get you to lean in and focus on what they have to say.

Body language signs to watch

While no two people are going to express themselves using the exact same body language, once you get in the habit of looking for them you will find enough similarities to allow you to at least make an educated guess as to what is going on in most scenarios. At the very least, you should be able to successfully determine how relaxed the other person is with the current state of the conversation.

This is an ideal place to start if you are planning on being assertive without being seen as aggressive as a comfortable person will see something as assertive while an uncomfortable person will see the same action as aggressive. Keeping an eye out for this type of body language will then allow you to change your approach at the moment to ensure that you can keep things from suddenly spiraling downhill.

While you can certainly read about personal body language cues, the best way to learn to spot the body language of others is via lots and lots of practice. Remember, mastering body language cues is a marathon, not a sprint, slow and steady wins the race.

Positive signs: The first thing you will want to do when it comes to determining the other party's comfort level is to allow them to set the amount of space between you. If they establish a friendly perimeter and don't use anything to shield themselves from the conversation then you can confidently try to be assertive as you can be fairly confident you and the other party are already on the same page. Don't forget to clock the amount of space that was between you at the start, however, and also keep an eye out for any barriers that artificially create a set amount of space between you.

The next best indicator of the other party's general level of feeling towards you is going to be the direction that their feet are currently facing. While it may seem silly, it is a fact that most people will point their feet towards the direction of the person they agree with in a conversation. Likewise, if you sneak a peek and find that their feet are facing the opposite direction then it is time to do something drastic if you don't want to come off as overly aggressive.

If you and the other person are both standing, then a titled head is a surefire sign that they agree with what you are saying, which is a signal that is mirrored in the hands behind the head posture if you are both sitting. When looking at the other person's face, the first thing you are going to want to keep an eye on is the obvious, smiling and laughter are the best, though a general calm attitude is also a mark in the win column. Depending on the type of interaction, a brief positive physical contact is always a good sign. Nine times out of 10, a physical contact indicates a greenlight, regardless of how brief the contact itself might be.

Negative signs: While the signs a person might express are going to vary based on how uncomfortable or angry they are in the current situation; these red flags are often going to be quite similar between different individuals which means being aware of what to look for is a surefire way to ensure you can fight back against the feeling as effectively as possible. One of the most commonly seen signs of discomfort is going to be a habitual rubbing or touching of the back of the neck, with the rate and frequency of the rubbing directly reflecting the amount of discomfort that is being felt. While this might seem like a fairly conscious, forced, gesture, the truth of the matter is that this area is home to a large number of nerve endings and rubbing it actually lowers the heart rate. If the other party is wearing a tie or necklace, then playing with it will indicate the same.

Rubbing indicates discomfort on any part of the body, in fact, not just on the back of the neck but on the forehead, hair, eyes, lips and face as well. Rubbing of the hands is a common sign if you and the other person are sitting and rubbing of the legs means the same if you are standing. Finally, you will find that puffing of the cheeks or loud exhaling are also a surefire sign that the other person is uncomfortable with some aspect of the current conversation and you will need to assuage them to ensure you can manage to be assertive effectively.

Step 9: Practice Assertive Body Language

In order to ensure you have truly mastered the art of appropriate body language, it is crucial that you spend as much time considering the nonverbal cues you are expressing to others as well as what they are telling you. Walking the line between being assertive in a negative way and being the assertive person everyone loves is difficult and locking down what your body language will ensure that one more piece of the puzzle is in place.

Studies show that two minutes of conversation is all it takes for a negative impression to form that can take months, if not years, to shake. Essentially what this means is that if you want to the person you are speaking with to form the right type of opinion of you then you will need to think carefully about how you approach a topic where you need to be assertive and the following can help.

Perfect posture: Regardless of the task at hand, you will come out looking better while doing it if your back is straight and your shoulders are squared. When you speak, make sure your eyes are straight ahead, showing that you are ready to face the consequences of your statement. This shows the person you are speaking with that you are ready to face the conversation head on, but also that you are looking for a positive interaction. While keeping the above in mind, you should also strive to look relaxed as possible as if you look tense then it appears as though you are looking for a fight which is going to make an assertive suggestion sound like a command. Looking relaxed will also make you look more confident, making it even more likely that your point will be positively received.

Whenever you are speaking with someone face to face, it is important to always make an effort to physically align your body with theirs as much as you can, within reason. At the very least, this means that if they are standing or sitting then you should follow suit, but it also means that you need to plant your feet at shoulder width as this indicates you have nothing to hide. As an added bonus it will also ensure you look more relaxed, while also actually ensuring that you retain information more easily.

While you are in the midst of your conversation, you are also going to need to make a habit of slowly copying the mannerisms and gestures of the person you are speaking to. This will help to put them at ease and ensure they are more likely to agree with any assertive suggestions you might make. You will know that you have them convinced of your way of thinking when you can switch the paradigm and take on your own mannerisms that the other person then subconsciously mimics.

Arms and hands: The most important rule when it comes to what to do with your hands and arms is that the action appears as normal as possible. If you find yourself overthinking these mannerisms then you will destroy their fluidity and it will make them feel awkward and forced. If you aren't a big gesturer by nature, it is not something that you need to force as an awkward gesture is going to be worse than no gesture at all.

Much like with your posture, your goal here should be to always look as relaxed as possible. If you are asking for something reasonable while being assertive, after all, then there is nothing for you to be nervous about. Above all else, however, it is very important that you avoid standing with your arms crossed unless you want to project a very specific message. This pose is known to signal one thing and one thing only, you are not interested in achieving a group consensus of any sort and are only interested in promoting your own agenda.

When it comes to being appropriately assertive, you are going to want to stand with your arms hanging naturally at your sides. This will show those you are speaking with that you are looking to come to a true consensus and that you are willing to listen to what they have to say, not just get your own way. When standing with your arms at your sides, be sure to avoid standing with balled fists; if you are sitting be sure to avoid sitting with both of your palms flat on the table. Both of these show that you don't agree with the current topic of conversation or that it is making you angry, neither of which is beneficial if you are looking for everyone to leave happy.

If you are not naturally particularly expressive with your hand movements, it is still vital that you understand how important a good handshake is when it comes to making an appropriate impression that you can capitalize on when the time comes to get what you need from the conversation. The perfect handshake is firm but not overly aggressive. Anything more over the top than this indicates that you are looking to dominate the other person and is almost certainly going to cause them to push back when you assert yourself. Likewise, if you let the other person dominate the handshake by going limp then it is possible they will feel as though they have already dominated you, making it even harder for you to be assertive when the time comes. It is also important to keep in mind that this is not the case across all cultures and to plan ahead if you don't know the local customs.

Mind your head: If you want to clearly indicate that you and the other person are on the same page, then nodding along with what they are saying is the ideal first step. You will also get similar results by mimicking their facial expressions, just don't get so caught up in doing so that you lose the thread of the conversation. If you laugh, make sure that it is clearly an appropriate time to do so and never laugh as a sign of nervousness. When used appropriately, laughter is a great way to break the ice or to start off a new conversation on the right foot, but only if done in a way that you know the other person will enjoy. It shows that you are fun to be around, agreeable and jovial, but it also indicates you are in sync with the other person and understand their wants and needs.

Consider how you sound: When you do speak, it is important that you use a confident, calm tone as this will naturally make those you are speaking with more interested in what you have to say. Additionally, you will need to ensure that the speed and volume of your speech are appropriate for your audience and the topic in question. It is also important that you banish all filler words from your speech as words like "um or "like" will only make you sound as though you don't know what you are talking about or that you are unsure of yourself, two things you can't have if you hope to appear assertive. Finally, it is important that you enunciate clearly as this shows that you value what you have to say and will make other people more likely to do the same.

Avoid this type of body language
While there are plenty of body language options that can improve your case with the person you are speaking with if you aren't careful you can stumble into just as many opportunities to ruin your chance to be assertive effectively beyond repair. Do yourself a favor and keep the following out of your interpersonal interactions at all times, you will be glad you did.

Head tilting: Regardless of why you may feel the need to do so, it is vital that you avoid looking down your nose at the person you are speaking with if you want them to remain on your side. The phrase "look down your nose" exists because people feel as tough taking this pose is akin to saying you are better than they are which is never a productive place to start a conversation from. If you make the mistake of using this type of body language while you are having an argument with someone then you can virtually guarantee that they will end up coming down against your point even harder than before. The better choice is to instead make eye contact with the other person about 50 percent of the time while you are speaking and even more than that while they are speaking to show that you really value their input.

Don't have ants in your pants: When you are working to be assertive effectively, it is important to do whatever it takes to ensure you don't fidget, even if it is something you would do naturally anyway. A majority of the time, people find those who are fidgeting to be untrustworthy, and you never want to appear to anything other than the best of the best when you strive to be assertive.

This extended to things like touching your nose and eyes; as well as bouncing your leg or tapping your feet, cracking your knuckles, biting your nails or scratching at one arm. This doesn't mean you should not move at all, however, as you should still be using positive body language to indicate that you are following what the other person is saying and agree with their general ideas.

Step 10: Fake It Until You Make It

Here's the real secret to faking assertiveness, if you act as though you are confident and assertive in whatever it is that you are doing then those around you will naturally assume you are both of those things. For the other person in the conversation, there is no difference between a you who is confident and assertive and a you who is only pretending to be those things which means that pretending is a great way to build up your self-confidence in the early days before being assertive is something that comes as second nature to you.

If you don't think it can possibly be that easy, give it a try, you will be surprised at the results. What's more, every successful interaction will make it easier to have self-confidence in the next until eventually, you will be assertive all of the time no matter what. Once you have found the ability to be assertive, even in the face of adversity, you will realize it is much easier to be empowered, no matter what. Until you get to the point where you don't need to fake it any more, get started with the following tips.

Mimic your self-confidence idol: If at first, you are unsure how to react in a given scenario the way a person with lots of self-confidence would, stop and take a moment to picture the most confident person you know. From there all you will need to do is ask yourself how that person would act in the situation you now find yourself in. Don't be vague in your assumptions, it helps to get specific. Ask yourself how they move, how they respond to others, what their body language suggests and what their speech patterns are like and then do your best to follow their lead.

Look the part: When you are projecting self-confidence about your assertiveness that you don't really feel, it is important to act the part. For starters, try and always walk as though you have somewhere you really need to be. To get the right look, consider increasing your walking speed by about 25 percent. You don't have time for a regular speed, you are confident you know where you are going at that the people who are waiting for you value your input.

When you do have to stop and speak with someone it is important to avoid slumping your shoulders or slouching while you or the other person are speaking. It is also important to always make eye contact for at least 75 percent of every conversation. During conversations make it a point of compliment other people as self-confident people often see the best in others, as well as themselves. Compliments are also an excellent way to begin a conversation as it guarantees you already have the other person's interest.

Consider the version of yourself that other people see: Those who project assertiveness tend to be perceived by others as happier, more outgoing and all around friendlier. As such, if you want others to see you as a more assertive person, start by always introducing yourself to others first and smiling regularly. Always participate fully in any activities that involve the group as a whole and the group will naturally think of you as a confident person. Taking the time to always introduce yourself to new people directly will let others know that you are an individual who is sure of themselves and thus deserves respect.

Speak appropriately: While those who lack the ability to be assertive on demand tend to rarely speak up, even when confronted directly, this doesn't mean that those who are assertive do the opposite. In fact, speaking too much can actually hurt your case as much as not expressing yourself at all can. If you speak too much, then you run the risk of coming off as if you aren't suggesting a solution as much as you are looking for approval, likely because you don't believe that your solution is good enough to stand on its own.

If speaking too much or too little can both backfire, then it is important to instead speak up and interject your thoughts in a manner that is confident and to otherwise remain silent, secure in the fact that you are a valuable member of the team. Regardless of how sure you are of the option you have come up with, all you need to do is to pretend as though it is the only logical choice and you will be surprised at how often most people get on board with the idea. Remember, most people are actually using the time you are speaking to consider what they themselves are going to say next you can use this to your advantage and appear wise enough for other people to fall into line.

If you find yourself with the need to be assertive in a less formal setting, you are going to want to avoid the mistake of talking about yourself more than is necessary. At the same time, you aren't going to want to deflect any compliments that do come your way as doing so only shows that you don't believe you are worthy of the compliments that are being sent in your direction. On the contrary, if you spend too much time talking about all of the great things you have done in the past, you will come off as though you are constantly looking for validation from others. If the conversation turns towards your accomplishments, feel free to discuss as needed, just don't go overboard and you will be fine.

If you find yourself in a conversation with someone who is constantly cutting you off, then it is important that you exercise your assertiveness by sticking up for yourself as this is what anyone with the confidence to be assertive would do. This will make it clear to all involved that you are someone who values your thoughts and opinions which makes it more likely that other people will as well.

Conclusion

Thank you for making it through to the end of *Assertiveness Training: 10 Simple Steps How to Become The Person You Meant to Be, Self-Expression, Speak up, Stand Up For Yourself Without Being Arrogant And Take Control of Your Own Life*, let's hope it was informative and able to provide you with all of the tools you need to achieve your goals, whatever it is that they may be. Just because you've finished this book doesn't mean there is nothing left to learn on the topic, expanding your horizons is the only way to find the mastery you seek.

Above all else, it is important to remember that being assertive is a skill which means that like any other skill it will only ever improve with practice. While the first time you find yourself standing up and speaking out will likely be difficult to power through and a little bit scary, it is important to understand that the second time will be easier and the third time even easier than that until eventually, you are able to be assertive without even giving it a second thought.

This is not to say that it will happen overnight, however, as working through the steps above will take some time to complete properly. This is why it is important to not go into the process expecting to be an expert at asserting yourself tomorrow or even next week. Becoming an expert at being assertive takes time and dedication if you hope to make real long-lasting changes in your life. Becoming assertive is a marathon, not a sprint which means that slow and steady wins the race.

www.ingramcontent.com/pod-product-compliance
Lightning Source LLC
Chambersburg PA
CBHW071316080526
44587CB00018B/3250